ABRAHAM

HEARING GOD'S CALL

JACK KUHATSCHEK

9 STUDIES
FOR INDIVIDUALS
OR GROUPS

Life
Builder
Study

INTER-VARSITY PRESS
36 Causton Street, London SW1P 4ST, England
Email: ivp@ivpbooks.com
Website: www.ivpbooks.com

Originally published in the United States of America in the LifeGuide® Bible Studies series in 2004 by InterVarsity Press, Downers Grove, Illinois
First published in Great Britain by Scripture Union in 2005
This edition published in Great Britain by Inter-Varsity Press 2021

British Library Cataloguing-in-Publication Data
A catalogue record for this book is available from the British Library.

ISBN: 978-1-78359-888-5

Printed in Great Britain by Ashford Colour Press Ltd, Gosport, Hampshire

Produced on paper from sustainable sources.

Inter-Varsity Press publishes Christian books that are true to the Bible and that communicate the gospel, develop discipleship and strengthen the church for its mission in the world.

IVP originated within the Inter-Varsity Fellowship, now the Universities and Colleges Christian Fellowship, a student movement connecting Christian Unions in universities and colleges throughout Great Britain, and a member movement of the International Fellowship of Evangelical Students. Website: www.uccf.org.uk. That historic association is maintained, and all senior IVP staff and committee members subscribe to the UCCF Basis of Faith.

Contents

Getting the Most Out of *Abraham*

The Secret Garden by Frances Hodgson Burnett tells the story of a young orphan girl named Mary Lennox who goes to live with her maternal uncle, Archibald Craven, at Misselthwaite Manor in Yorkshire, England. "Everybody said she was the most disagreeable-looking child ever seen. It was true, too. She had a little thin face and a little thin body, thin light hair and a sour expression." Mary was extremely spoiled, self-centered and bad tempered. She loved no one, and no one loved her.

Then one day while playing outside Mary discovers the door to a walled garden, a secret garden, that no one had entered for ten years.

"It was the sweetest, most mysterious-looking place any one could imagine. The high walls which shut it in were covered with the leafless stems of climbing roses which were so thick that they were matted together. Mary Lennox knew they were roses because she had seen a great many roses in India. All the ground was covered with grass of a wintry brown and out of it grew clumps of bushes which were surely rosebushes if they were alive. . . . Mary had thought it must be different from other gardens which had not been left all by themselves so long; and indeed it was different from any other place she had ever seen in her life."

Mary and a boy named Dickon begin lovingly to care for the garden. They clear away the grass and weeds that are smothering the plants trying to push up from the earth. They prune the rosebushes, plant seeds and bulbs, and spend every waking minute in the secret garden.

When spring arrives, a miracle happens. Both the garden and Mary begin to blossom and grow until there is a profusion of roses, daffodils, crocuses and every other variety of flower, and the sickly, sour-faced girl becomes healthy and radiant. At first the children think this is all the result of Magic, but then Dickon's mother explains that the Magic has a name, and together they sing the doxology: "Praise God from whom all blessings flow."

The book of Genesis tells the story of a man named Abraham, who lives in a barren land of pagans, idols and immorality. Then one day he meets the Lord, the "God from whom all blessings flow," who promises to make Abraham flourish and become fruitful beyond his wildest imagination. Slowly, over a period of twenty-five years, a miracle begins to happen. This former pagan gradually becomes a man of God; this liar and deceiver becomes full of truth and wisdom; and the tender, delicate faith Abraham has at the beginning of the story grows stronger and more resilient until it becomes a model of faith for generations to come—and for us today.

This LifeBuilder introduces us to the life of Abraham, the man of faith and the friend of God. In nine sessions we too will learn how to patiently trust God and wait for the fulfillment of his amazing promises to us. We will discover that all the blessings we experience in life are the result of the divine Magic, which has a name: "Praise God from whom all blessings flow."

Suggestions for Individual Study

1. As you begin each study, pray that God will speak to you through his Word.

2. Read the introduction to the study and respond to the personal reflection question or exercise. This is designed to help you focus on God and on the theme of the study.

3. Each study deals with a particular passage—so that you can delve into the author's meaning in that context. Read and reread the passage to be studied. The questions are written using the language of the New International Version, so you may wish to use that version of the Bible. The New Revised Standard Version is also recommended.

4. This is an inductive Bible study, designed to help you discover for yourself what Scripture is saying. The study includes three types of questions. *Observation* questions ask about the basic facts: who, what, when, where and how. *Interpretation* questions delve into the meaning of the passage. *Application* questions help you discover the implications of the text for growing in Christ. These three keys unlock the treasures of Scripture.

Write your answers to the questions in the spaces provided or in a personal journal. Writing can bring clarity and deeper understanding of yourself and of God's Word.

5. It might be good to have a Bible dictionary handy. Use it to look up any unfamiliar words, names or places.

6. Use the prayer suggestion to guide you in thanking God for what you have learned and to pray about the applications that have come to mind.

7. You may want to go on to the suggestion under "Now or Later," or you may want to use that idea for your next study.

Suggestions for Members of a Group Study

1. Come to the study prepared. Follow the suggestions for individual study mentioned above. You will find that careful preparation will greatly enrich your time spent in group discussion.

2. Be willing to participate in the discussion. The leader of your group will not be lecturing. Instead, he or she will be encouraging the members of the group to discuss what they have learned. The leader will be asking the questions that are found in this guide.

3. Stick to the topic being discussed. Your answers should be based on the verses which are the focus of the discussion and not on outside authorities such as commentaries or speakers. These studies focus on a particular passage of Scripture. Only rarely should you refer to other portions of the Bible. This allows for everyone to participate in in-depth study on equal ground.

4. Be sensitive to the other members of the group. Listen attentively when they describe what they have learned. You may be surprised by their insights! Each question assumes a variety of answers. Many questions do not have "right" answers, particularly questions that aim at meaning or application. Instead the questions push us to explore the passage more thoroughly.

When possible, link what you say to the comments of others. Also, be affirming whenever you can. This will encourage some of the more hesitant members of the group to participate.

5. Be careful not to dominate the discussion. We are sometimes so eager to express our thoughts that we leave too little opportunity for others to respond. By all means participate! But allow others to also.

6. Expect God to teach you through the passage being discussed and through the other members of the group. Pray that you will have an enjoyable and profitable time together, but also that as a result of the study you will find ways that you can take action individually and/or as a group.

7. Remember that anything said in the group is considered confidential and should not be discussed outside the group unless specific permission is given to do so.

8. If you are the group leader, you will find additional suggestions at the back of the guide.

1

Hearing God's Call

In J. R. R. Tolkien's classic tale *The Lord of the Rings*, a hobbit named Frodo is told he must leave his comfortable home in the Shire and travel to a distant land. When the initial shock wears off, he comments, "Of course, I have sometimes thought of going away, but I imagined that as a kind of holiday, a series of adventures like Bilbo's or better, ending in peace. But this would mean exile, a flight from danger into danger. . . . As for where I am going, it would be difficult to give that away, for I have no clear idea myself, yet . . . where am I to go? And by what shall I steer? What is to be my quest? . . . I feel very small, and very uprooted, and well—desperate."*

GROUP DISCUSSION. Describe a time when you were asked to leave your comfort zone and do something unfamiliar and difficult.

PERSONAL REFLECTION. Why do you think God sometimes asks us to leave our comfort zones?

In Genesis 12, God commands Abram to leave everything that

is familiar, comfortable and secure in order to fulfill God's plan for his life. *Read Genesis 12.*

---

1. What would be difficult about leaving your country, your people and your extended family in order to go to an unknown destination (v. 1)?

---

2. What are the various facets of the promises God makes to Abram (vv. 2-3)?

---

3. In what ways does God call us to give up our comfort and security in the present in order to embrace his promises for the future?

---

4. Clearly the author of Genesis isn't interested in the details of Abram's journey: "They set out for the land of Canaan, and they arrived there." What is the primary focus of verses 4-5, and why? (See also Hebrews 11:8.)

---

5. In verses 6-7 what two key statements seem to clash with each other and create tension?

6. How do you typically respond when God's promises seem to clash with present realities?

7. What evidence do we see that Abram resolved this tension in his own heart and mind (vv. 7-9)?

8. In verses 10-16 how do the changes in Abram's life and circumstances threaten both his faith in God and the promises God made to him?

9. Why do you think God punishes Pharaoh, who acted in ignorance, instead of Abram, who acted in disobedience and unbelief (vv. 17-20)?

10. What does Genesis 12 teach you about the practical realities of living by faith?

Three times in this passage we are told that Abram built an altar to the Lord and worshiped him (12:7-8; 13:4). Take time now to thank God for his promises to you and his faithfulness in your life.

Now or Later

Biblical scholars often see parallels between Abram's time in Egypt and Israel's stay there prior to the exodus. Read the following texts. What similarities do you see in these two accounts?

Genesis 12:10 and 47:4
Genesis 12:12-15 and Exodus 1:11-14
Genesis 12:17 and Exodus 7:14—12:30
Genesis 12:16, 20 and Exodus 12:33-36
Genesis 13:3 and Exodus 17:1
Genesis 13:3-4 and Exodus 15:17**

---

*J. R. R. Tolkien, *The Lord of the Rings* (Great Britain: HarperCollins, 1994), pp. 61, 64-65.

**Bruce K. Waltke, *Genesis* (Grand Rapids, Mich.: Zondervan, 2001), p. 217.

2

Lift Up Your Eyes

Genesis 13

In a TV rerun of *The Little Rascals*, twin boys decide to share a candy bar. One of the twins breaks the candy bar in two pieces and hands the other the shorter piece. When his brother complains that his piece is shorter, the first twin takes it back, holds it up to his own, and then bites off the longer piece until it is the same size as the shorter one. His brother seems completely satisfied with this procedure, and the two of them eat together in peace.

My mother had a much better procedure for dividing a candy bar, twinkie or any similar treasure. One of us would be allowed to divide the candy bar, but the other got to select the piece he wanted. It worked every time!

GROUP DISCUSSION. How do adults sometimes fight over "what's mine" and "what's yours"?

PERSONAL REFLECTION. When have you demanded (or been tempted to demand) your rights to something someone else wanted?

In Genesis 13, Abram and Lot begin to crowd and quarrel with each other over where they each should live and graze their flocks. *Read Genesis 13.*

---

1. In what ways does this passage describe the great wealth of Abram and Lot?

---

2. What factors contribute to the growing conflict between the herdsmen—and between Abram and Lot (vv. 5-8)?

---

3. God had already promised the land of Canaan to Abram (Genesis 12:7). Why then do you think Abram is willing to give up his rights—including the fertile plain surrounding the Jordan River that looked like the Garden of Eden (Genesis 13:8-11)?

---

4. Do you think Abram's offer was an act of foolishness, which threatened God's promise, or an act of faith, which trusted God to fulfill his promise? Explain why.

5. How can we know when it's best to demand and even fight for our rights versus giving in and trusting God to provide for us?

6. What indications are there in verses 10-13 that Lot chose the best land but the worst place to live (see also Genesis 19:22-25)?

7. In what ways can the lure of affluence blind us to more important values?

8. Compare the promises God makes to Abram in verses 14-17 with the earlier versions of the promises (Genesis 12:1-3, 7). How does the wording in chapter 13 intensify what was said before?

9. By the time we get to the New Testament, how has the promise to Abram reached far beyond what he might have imagined (Galatians 3:9, 14)?

---

10. In what ways can you follow Abram's example of trusting God to fulfill his promises to you?

Take time to thank God for the incredible promises we have through faith in Christ. Ask him for grace to trust him more each day.

Now or Later

Read and reflect on Galatians 3:6-29. How do these verses advance your understanding of the promises to Abraham and how they apply to you today?

3

Going to Battle

Dr. Seuss wrote a children's story called *Yertle the Turtle*, which describes a self-absorbed king of a little pond on the faraway Island of Sala-ma-Sond. Yertle boasted that he was king of all he could see, but one day he decided he couldn't see enough: "'This throne that I sit on is too, too low down. It ought to be *higher!*' he said with a frown. 'If I could sit high, how much greater I'd be! What a king! I'd be ruler of all I could see!'"

In order to expand his horizons and power, Yertle ordered all of the turtles in his pond to climb on each other's backs so that they could become his new and higher throne. From this lofty perch, Yertle swelled with pride and feelings of self-importance. "'All mine!' Yertle cried. . . . 'Oh, marvelous me! For I am the ruler of all that I see!'"

Then one day, from the bottom of Yertle's throne, an insignificant turtle named Mack burped and toppled Yertle headlong in a downward plunge into the pond. Dr. Seuss concludes the story by saying, "And today the great Yertle, that Marvelous he, is King of the Mud. That is all he can see."*

GROUP DISCUSSION. A well-known proverb says that "pride

goes before a fall." Why do you think that is often the case?

PERSONAL REFLECTION. When has your pride resulted in personal humiliation?

In Genesis 14 the kings of the east and the kings of Canaan encounter the King of all the earth and his representative, Abram. *Read Genesis 14.*

---

1. How many times does the word *king* appear in this chapter?

Why do you think that word is so often repeated?

---

2. How does your impression of royalty compare to or contrast with what you see here?

---

3. How does the author of Genesis emphasize the power of the four kings of the east (vv. 1-12)?

4. Having described the power of the kings of the east, what does the author of Genesis want us to know about Abram from the events in verses 13-16?

5. Melchizedek appears as if out of nowhere and then just as quickly disappears from Scripture (vv. 18-20). What does Scripture reveal about this mysterious person (Psalm 110; Hebrews 7:1-3)?

6. How do Melchizedek's and Abram's words and actions put the previous battle into perspective?

7. In what ways can we honor "God Most High" for the blessings and victories he gives us?

8. How does Abram's encounter with the king of Sodom (vv. 21-24) contrast with his encounter with Melchizedek?

9. Abram refuses the king of Sodom's offer "so that you will never be able to say, 'I made Abram rich'" (v. 23). Why is it so important for us to realize that ultimately God alone is our provider and king?

10. In what ways has God provided for you recently?

Take time to thank and honor God for his gracious gifts.

Now or Later

Although Melchizedek is mentioned only briefly in Genesis, how does he reflect the coming of Jesus, the ultimate King and Priest (Hebrews 6:19—7:10)?

---

*Dr. Seuss, *Yertle the Turtle and Other Stories* (New York: Random House, 1950).

4

The Covenant

When I was a boy, one of my favorite "cowboy and Indian" shows on TV was called *Broken Arrow,* starring Michael Ansara as the Apache chief Cochise and John Lupton as Indian agent Tom Jeffords. In one episode the two men decide to become blood brothers. Using a large hunting knife, they cut themselves and lash their hands together so that their blood can flow as one, forming a permanent bond between them.

After watching the show, my best friend and I decided that we too should become blood brothers. But instead of using a large hunting knife, which seemed excessive, we decided to take the easy way out. We found a sewing needle, pricked the ends of our fingers, pressed them together for about thirty seconds, and we were done!

GROUP DISCUSSION. In what ways do people in our culture use symbols or rituals to demonstrate their commitment to each other?

PERSONAL REFLECTION. How do you demonstrate your commitment to your best friend or spouse?

In Genesis 15 Abram believes God's promises, and the Lord establishes his covenant with Abram. *Read Genesis 15.*

1. Verse 1 begins with the reassurance, "Do not be afraid, Abram." How do Abram's questions in this chapter help us understand his fears?

2. Why would being childless (v. 2) have been a major concern for Abram or anyone in his culture?

3. Why would it have required faith to believe God's promises in verses 4-5?

4. In what ways do Abram's faith and God's response (v. 6) become a model for us today (see Romans 4:18-25)?

5. In verse 7 the focus shifts from Abram's offspring to his possession of the Promised Land. If Abram already believes the Lord (v. 6), why do you think he seeks further assurance (v. 8)?

6. When two people in ancient Near Eastern cultures made a covenant, they both walked between the carcasses of animals, signifying that if they broke the covenant they should suffer the same fate as the animals. What is the significance of the fact that only the Lord passes between the pieces (v. 17)?

7. Sandwiched between Abram's preparation for the covenant ceremony (vv. 9-11) and the actual ceremony itself (vv. 17-21) is a prophecy about Israel's enslavement in Egypt. During that enslavement, how would Israel's fears, questions and need for assurance parallel those of Abram?

How might they have been comforted and encouraged by reading this account?

8. What fears, questions and need for assurance do you have about God fulfilling his promises to you?

---

9. Because we are in Christ, we too are heirs of the covenant God made with Abram (see Galatians 3:15-18). How then can this chapter increase your confidence in God's faithfulness to you?

Bring to the Lord your fears, questions and need for assurance about the future. Thank him for his great promises and unchanging faithfulness.

Now or Later

Throughout the Bible people gain confidence about the future by remembering God's faithfulness in the past. Write down some of the ways God has demonstrated his faithfulness to you. How can these things strengthen your faith in God and increase your hope for the future?

5

Do-It-Yourself Religion

Patience is a virtue we spend our whole lives trying to truly learn. Here is one account of how patience feels.

I remembered one morning when I discovered a cocoon in the bark of a tree, just as the butterfly was making a hole in its case and preparing to come out. I waited a while, but it was too long appearing and I was impatient. I bent over it, and breathed on it to warm it. I warmed it as quickly as I could and the miracle began to happen before my eyes, faster than life. The case opened, the butterfly started slowly crawling out and I shall never forget my horror when I saw how its wings were folded back and crumpled; the wretched butterfly tried with its whole trembling body to unfold them. Bending over it, I tried to help it with my breath. In vain. It needed to be hatched out patiently and the unfolding of the wings be a gradual process in the sun. Now it was too late. My breath had forced the butterfly to appear, all crumpled, before its time. It struggled desperately and, a few seconds later, died in the palm of my hand. I realize today that . . . we should not hurry, we should not be impatient, but we should confidently obey the eternal rhythm.*

GROUP DISCUSSION. What examples can you think of where trying to rush something to completion ends up damaging or destroying it?

PERSONAL REFLECTION. In what areas do you need to learn to wait more patiently for God to work?

In Genesis 16 Abram and Sarai become impatient with God's delayed promise and decide to take matters into their own hands. *Read Genesis 16.*

1. What tensions, conflicts and emotions did you observe as you read this passage?

2. Abram and Sarai had waited ten years for God to give them children (see Genesis 12:4; 16:3). What might have convinced Sarai to devise this plan to help God fulfill his promise (vv. 1-2)?

3. Why do you think Abram, the man of faith, agreed to this scheme (vv. 3-4)?

4. Why are we tempted to blame God (v. 2) and assume that he has said no when, in fact, he has said wait?

---

5. Why do you think Sarai shifts the blame to Abram (vv. 4-5) when her clever plan backfires?

---

6. How would you evaluate Abram's "solution" to the problem (v. 6)?

---

7. What potential dangers do we face when we stop trusting God and try to take matters into our own hands?

---

8. In verses 9-14 the scene focuses on Hagar and her son. Why do you think so much space is devoted to a maidservant and her unborn child?

9. What do verses 9-14 reveal about the Lord?

10. How does it help you to know that the Lord sees, hears and responds when you suffer?

Thank God for his compassion and care in your life. Ask him for strength to trust him when his answers to your prayers seem delayed.

Now or Later

This is the only passage in ancient Near Eastern literature where a deity calls a woman by name. It is also the only passage in the Bible where a human gives God a name. How does this intimate look at Hagar, the maidservant, help you to better understand God's love and grace?

---

*Nikos Kazantzakis, *Zorba the Greek,* trans. Carl Wildman (New York: Scribner, 1996).

6

Confirming the Covenant

Throughout the late 1930s and early 1940s children gathered around the family radio every afternoon at 4:30 to listen to the program *Little Orphan Annie*. The announcer, Pierre Andre, would conclude each broadcast by inviting all club members to decipher a secret message that could only be understood by those who had an official Little Orphan Annie decoder ring. Yet the only way to become a club member and to receive the official decoder ring was by sending in twenty-five cents and the label from the inside of an Ovaltine lid.

A writer named Harris Akell describes what it was like to join this secret society: "After three agonizing weeks, the package bearing the decoder ring and official membership card finally arrived. That afternoon I could barely wait for the program to begin. Today's adventure was of no interest to me. All I could think about was the secret message. I was finally going to find out what these secret messages were. Finally, the adventure ended. Pierre Andre told everyone to take out their rings, and he announced the letters for that day's secret message: 'A4, A6, B2 . . .' I copied the code, letter by letter, onto a piece of paper so that I wouldn't miss any of them. When the last letter was announced, I took my ring in hand and started to decode my very first message as an official club member. This was exciting! The seemingly jumbled letters actually spelled a sentence. My hands shook with excitement. When I was through deciphering the message, I stopped to read it. As I read the message, I felt that I must have missed something, so I decoded the message again. But it still read the same: 'Drink your Ovaltine to grow big and strong and tune in to *Little Orphan Annie's* adventures every day at this same time.'" After decoding the message, the disappointed eight-year-old Askell mumbled, "With a secret message like that, no wonder Annie is an orphan."*

GROUP DISCUSSION. Thinking back to childhood or drawing on your current life, what are some ways you have proudly shown that you are a member of clubs or organizations?

PERSONAL REFLECTION. How do you respond to the truth that you are a special member of God's family?

In Genesis 17 God confirms his covenant with Abram and gives him a special sign of the covenant. Abram may have wished that the sign were a decoder ring or a secret handshake, but instead the Lord establishes the sign of circumcision. *Read Genesis 17.*

---

1. The structure of this passage is revealed by the expressions "As for me" (v. 4), "As for you" (v. 9) and "As for Sarai" (v. 15). What is the primary focus of each section?

2. Twenty-four years had passed since God first promised Abram that he would have children. After so many years of waiting for a child, how would you have felt about having your name changed from Abram ("exalted father") to Abraham ("father of many nations")?

3. God introduces himself as "God Almighty" (17:1)—the first time he has used this name in Genesis. How would the name give hope to Abraham?

How does the knowledge that you serve "God Almighty" give you hope in difficult circumstances?

4. As the Lord reaffirms his covenant with Abraham (vv. 4-8), which promises have been mentioned previously and which are new (see also Genesis 12:2-3; 15:4-21)?

5. Describe the details of Abraham's responsibility for keeping the covenant (vv. 9-14).

6. Up to this point the covenant had focused exclusively on Abraham and his offspring. Why then do you think the Lord commands that even "those who are not your offspring" (v. 12) should be circumcised?

In a small way, how does this command anticipate God's concern for those who are not physical descendants of Abraham—both then and today?

7. What is surprising, and even funny, about the Lord's promises about Sarah (vv. 15-18)?

8. How does the Lord get the last laugh by calling the promised son "Isaac," which means "one laughs" (see 17:17; 18:12; 21:6).

9. When has the Lord brought you either laughter or joy after doing something in your life that seemed impossible?

10. Up to this point Abraham may have thought that Ishmael was the son through whom the promises would be fulfilled (v. 18). How does the Lord clarify his plans for both Ishmael and Isaac (vv. 19-22)?

11. What impresses you about Abraham's response to God's commands (vv. 23-27)?

12. How can Abraham's obedience be a model for us as members of the new covenant through Jesus Christ?

Pray with honesty and gratitude to the God of the impossible.

Now or Later

Think about a situation you're facing that seems hopeless or impossible. Then take time to reflect on the fact that the Lord is "God Almighty." Offer your situation to the Lord in prayer, asking him to work a miracle in your life that will result in laughter and joyful thanksgiving.

*Good Old Days Magazine 37, no. 11 (2000).

7

Speaking
Face to Face

Genesis 18

In most stores in this country, the price of an item is clearly displayed and nonnegotiable. But in an oriental bazaar, a different custom is followed. If you find an item you're interested in buying, you make eye contact with the shop clerk, which signals to him that you would like to begin discussing the price. Then a time-honored process begins. The clerk will quote an inflated price merely as a starting point for haggling. He doesn't expect you to accept this price but rather to counter with your own price, which is lower than he is likely to accept. Greg Cruey writes: "The sales clerk expects to quote you a price and then watch you act surprised (maybe even insulted) and offer to pay 25 or 30 percent of what the clerk quoted. Then it is the clerk's turn to act surprised or insulted. Eventually the two of you settle on a price—often about half of what the clerk started out asking for—and everyone parts company as friends."*

GROUP DISCUSSION. Describe a time when you haggled over the price of an item you wished to buy.

PERSONAL REFLECTION. When have you wanted to plead with God for something better than what he seemed to offer?

In Genesis 18 the Lord appears to Abraham in human form. During their time together the Lord announces both the birth of Isaac and the destruction of Sodom and Gomorrah. *Read Genesis 18:1-15.*

1. In what ways does Abraham show great hospitality to his three guests?

2. How does Abraham's hospitality also demonstrate his godly character?

3. In verses 9-15 the focus of the conversation shifts to Sarah and the Lord's promise of a son. Humanly speaking, what good reasons did Sarah have for doubting and even laughing at the announcement she overheard?

4. Why do you think the Lord not only reveals her thoughts and her sin but also challenges her limited perspective?

5. What situation are you facing that seems either extremely difficult or impossible?

How does it help you to know that nothing is too hard for the Lord?

---

6. *Read Genesis 18:16-33.* In verse 17 the Lord asks, "Shall I hide from Abraham what I am about to do?" How do the statements in verses 18-19 help to determine the Lord's decision?

---

7. Throughout this chapter the Lord reveals himself in very human ways: he appears as a man (v. 2), he decides to investigate whether the claims about Sodom and Gomorrah are really true (vv. 20-21), and he enters into a very unusual dialogue with Abraham (vv. 22-33). Why do you think the Creator of heaven and earth would do such things?

How does the Lord's way of revealing himself to Abraham culminate in Jesus Christ?

8. The dialogue between Abraham and the Lord (vv. 23-33) seems to portray Abraham as more just, compassionate and merciful than God himself. Why do you think the Lord allows this strange role reversal?

---

9. In what ways are our prayers today similar to the dialogue between Abraham and the Lord?

---

10. When have you pleaded with God in prayer with the intensity and compassion shown by Abraham?

Thank God for the fact that he invites us to wrestle with him in prayer.

Now or Later

Think of someone in your life who desperately needs God's mercy and grace. Commit yourself to praying for them this week the way Abraham prayed for Sodom and Gomorrah. Begin by praying for them now.

---

*Greg Cruey, "Haggling," <http://goasia.about.com/library/weekly/aa071499a.htm>.

8

Receiving
the Promise

Creating a great instrument takes time and patience. Master violin makers look for the oldest wood they can find, which may be salvaged from a covered bridge built in 1866 in New Hampshire or a 150-year-old table discovered in Alaska. When wood ages, it dries and becomes more dense and resonant. After the fronts and backs of the violins have been carved from the antique wood, the craftsman dries them in the sun at intervals for a year. Even then the aging process is not complete. Finished violins must be played to reach their potential because playing causes the wood to vibrate and become more flexible, which improves their sound. The oldest and best violins, such as those made by Antonio Stradivari or Guiseppe Guarneri, can cost between $200,000 and $3.5 million, depending on their condition and history.*

GROUP DISCUSSION. What similarities do you see between a master violinmaker creating a great instrument and the Creator shaping and molding our character?

PERSONAL REFLECTION. In what ways do you become impatient with your personal and spiritual growth?

In Genesis 21 the long-awaited son is finally born. *Read Genesis 21:1-21.*

1. Which character in this narrative receives the greatest attention? Explain your answer.

2. How is the Lord's faithfulness emphasized in verses 1-2?

3. Twenty-five long years had passed since God first promised Abraham a son. How does the story of Abraham help you to trust God's faithfulness and believe his promises?

4. In what ways do verses 3-7 reveal Abraham's obedience and Sarah's delight?

5. How do the mood and focus of the story dramatically shift from verse 8 to verses 9-13?

6. What similarities do you see between the stories of Hagar and Ishmael in this chapter and chapter 16?

7. Although Isaac has been chosen and Ishmael rejected, how does the story of Hagar and Ishmael reveal God's compassion and care?

8. In Galatians 4:21-31 Paul claims that the stories of the two women and their sons illustrate the contrasts between the natural and the supernatural and between human effort and faith. In what ways do we continually face these two choices in our life with God?

In what way are you currently facing such a choice?

9. What does this chapter teach you about God, who is the primary character in every biblical narrative?

10. What part does the character of God have in shaping the choices you are making?

Take time now to thank God for his faithfulness, power and compassion in your life.

Now or Later

Read Galatians 4:21-31. How does Paul's retelling of the story shed new light on the drama in Genesis?

---

*Neil Grauer, "Heavenly Strings," <www.cigaraficionado.com/Cigar/CA_Feature/CA_Feature_Basic_Template/0,2344,597,00.html>; and Benjamin Helphand, "The Art of Making Violins," *The Aspen Times*, August 1998, <http://www.landon-violins.com/aspentimes.php>.

9

The Ultimate Test

Genesis 22:1-19

During the late 1950s two of the biggest TV shows were *The $64,000 Question* and *Twenty-One*. Entire families would gather around the television to watch amazing feats of mental gymnastics. Every week two contestants entered soundproof booths to answer seemingly impossible questions, such as "Was Paul Revere's horse a stallion or a mare?" Or, "What movie received the most Oscars in 1932?" Or, "What is the exact speed of sound under water?"

One of the best and brainiest contestants was a man named Charles Van Doren, who was a lecturer at Columbia and a member of one of the nation's most literary families. "His father was a Pulitzer-prizewinning poet and scholar; his mother was a novelist; his uncle, a famous historian; his aunt, editor of a respected book-review journal."*

When the dashing Van Doren finally beat out a nerdy guy named Herbie Stempel, the nation had a new hero. During his long winning streak, Van Doren won $129,000 and received 500 marriage proposals!

Then suddenly there were rumors of scandal. After an investigation, it was discovered that Van Doren and the other winners had been given the answers in advance. And if that wasn't enough help, they could simply listen through their headphones as someone backstage gave them clues.

The viewing audience was outraged. This wasn't a true test of mental ability. Any fourth-grader with one good ear could have answered those questions. If anything, it was a test of moral character, and both the contestants and the networks failed miserably.

GROUP DISCUSSION. Think of the hardest academic test you ever took. What made it so difficult?

PERSONAL REFLECTION. Think of a moral or spiritual test you faced in the past year. How well did you do, and why?

In Genesis 22, Abraham is a contestant on the biblical version of *The $64,000 Question*. He faces the most difficult and painful test of his life. But this test is real, and God doesn't give him the answers in advance. As we read this passage, we'll discover the most dramatic example of faith and obedience in the Old Testament. We'll also learn how Abraham can be a role model for us today. *Read Genesis 22:1-19.*

1. "Take your son," "your only son," "Isaac," "whom you love," "sacrifice him." How would each word or phrase in God's command to Abraham intensify the emotion, tension and potential anguish he might feel?

2. What would go through your heart and mind if God asked you to do such a thing? (Assume that you know God is doing the asking.)

3. In fact, we read nothing of Abraham's internal struggles. But how do his actions reveal his obedience and faith (vv. 3-8)?

4. Why must our obedience and faith go hand in hand? In other words, why is either one insufficient without the other?

5. How do the drama and tension in the story reach a climax in verses 9-12?

6. The God who knows everything says to Abraham in verse 12, "Now I know that you fear God, because you have not withheld from me your son, your only son." In what sense does God now know that Abraham fears him?

7. Why do you think that both Abraham and the author of Genesis repeatedly stress that "the Lord will provide" (vv. 8, 13-14)?

8. When our faith is tested, why is it essential for us to believe that God will provide for our needs?

9. How do God's lavish promises to Abraham in verses 15-18 parallel his earlier promises in Genesis 12:1-3; 13:14-17; and 15:1-21?

Why are these promises so often repeated through Abraham's story? (What are we to learn from them?)

10. In what ways are your faith and obedience being put to the test?

How can Abraham's example and experience encourage you to faithfully obey God?

Ask God to grow a strong faith within you.

Now or Later

One of the best ways to strengthen our faith is to read about others who have trusted God. Commit to reading one or more of the following classics of faith: *George Muller of Bristol, Hudson Taylor's Spiritual Secret, The Shadow of the Almighty, The Hiding Place* or *Joni*.

---

*Richard Schickel, "Barbarians at the Gate," *Time Domestic* 144, no. 12 (1994).

Leader's Notes

Leading a Bible discussion can be an enjoyable and rewarding experience. But it can also be *scary*—especially if you've never done it before. If this is your feeling, you're in good company. When God asked Moses to lead the Israelites out of Egypt, he replied, "O LORD, please send someone else to do it" (Ex 4:13). It was the same with Solomon, Jeremiah and Timothy, but God helped these people in spite of their weaknesses, and he will help you as well.

You don't need to be an expert on the Bible or a trained teacher to lead a Bible discussion. The idea behind these inductive studies is that the leader guides group members to discover for themselves what the Bible has to say. This method of learning will allow group members to remember much more of what is said than a lecture would.

These studies are designed to be led easily. As a matter of fact, the flow of questions through the passage from observation to interpretation to application is so natural that you may feel that the studies lead themselves. This study guide is also flexible. You can use it with a variety of groups—student, professional, neighborhood or church groups. Each study takes forty-five to sixty minutes in a group setting.

There are some important facts to know about group dynamics and encouraging discussion. The suggestions listed below should enable you to effectively and enjoyably fulfill your role as leader.

Preparing for the Study

1. Ask God to help you understand and apply the passage in your

own life. Unless this happens, you will not be prepared to lead others. Pray too for the various members of the group. Ask God to open your hearts to the message of his Word and motivate you to action.

2. Read the introduction to the entire guide to get an overview of the entire book and the issues which will be explored.

3. As you begin each study, read and reread the assigned Bible passage to familiarize yourself with it.

4. This study guide is based on the New International Version of the Bible. It will help you and the group if you use this translation as the basis for your study and discussion.

5. Carefully work through each question in the study. Spend time in meditation and reflection as you consider how to respond.

6. Write your thoughts and responses in the space provided in the study guide. This will help you to express your understanding of the passage clearly.

7. It might help to have a Bible dictionary handy. Use it to look up any unfamiliar words, names or places. (For additional help on how to study a passage, see chapter five of *How to Lead a LifeBuilder Study,* IVP, 2018.)

8. Consider how you can apply the Scripture to your life. Remember that the group will follow your lead in responding to the studies. They will not go any deeper than you do.

9. Once you have finished your own study of the passage, familiarize yourself with the leader's notes for the study you are leading. These are designed to help you in several ways. First, they tell you the purpose the study guide author had in mind when writing the study. Take time to think through how the study questions work together to accomplish that purpose. Second, the notes provide you with additional background information or suggestions on group dynamics for various questions. This information can be useful when people have difficulty understanding or answering a question. Third, the leader's notes can alert you to potential problems you may encounter during the study.

10. If you wish to remind yourself of anything mentioned in the leader's notes, make a note to yourself below that question in the study.

Leading the Study

1. Begin the study on time. Open with prayer, asking God to help the group to understand and apply the passage.

2. Be sure that everyone in your group has a study guide. Encourage the group to prepare beforehand for each discussion by reading the introduction to the guide and by working through the questions in the study.

3. At the beginning of your first time together, explain that these studies are meant to be discussions, not lectures. Encourage the members of the group to participate. However, do not put pressure on those who may be hesitant to speak during the first few sessions. You may want to suggest the following guidelines to your group.

☐ Stick to the topic being discussed.

☐ Your responses should be based on the verses which are the focus of the discussion and not on outside authorities such as commentaries or speakers.

☐ These studies focus on a particular passage of Scripture. Only rarely should you refer to other portions of the Bible. This allows for everyone to participate in in-depth study on equal ground.

☐ Anything said in the group is considered confidential and will not be discussed outside the group unless specific permission is given to do so.

☐ We will listen attentively to each other and provide time for each person present to talk.

☐ We will pray for each other.

4. Have a group member read the introduction at the beginning of the discussion.

5. Every session begins with a group discussion question. The question or activity is meant to be used before the passage is read. The question introduces the theme of the study and encourages group members to begin to open up. Encourage as many members as possible to participate, and be ready to get the discussion going with your own response.

This section is designed to reveal where our thoughts or feelings need to be transformed by Scripture. That is why it is especially important not to read the passage before the discussion question is asked. The passage will tend to color the honest reactions people would otherwise give because they are, of course, supposed to think the way the Bible does.

You may want to supplement the group discussion question with an icebreaker to help people to get comfortable. See the community section of the *Small Group Starter Kit* (IVP, 1995) for more ideas.

You also might want to use the personal reflection question with your group. Either allow a time of silence for people to respond individually or discuss it together.

6. Have a group member (or members if the passage is long) read aloud the passage to be studied. Then give people several minutes to read the passage again silently so that they can take it all in.

7. Question 1 will generally be an overview question designed to briefly survey the passage. Encourage the group to look at the whole passage, but try to avoid getting sidetracked by questions or issues that will be addressed later in the study.

8. As you ask the questions, keep in mind that they are designed to be used just as they are written. You may simply read them aloud. Or you may prefer to express them in your own words.

There may be times when it is appropriate to deviate from the study guide. For example, a question may have already been answered. If so, move on to the next question. Or someone may raise an important question not covered in the guide. Take time to discuss it, but try to keep the group from going off on tangents.

9. Avoid answering your own questions. If necessary, repeat or rephrase them until they are clearly understood. Or point out something you read in the leader's notes to clarify the context or meaning. An eager group quickly becomes passive and silent if they think the leader will do most of the talking.

10. Don't be afraid of silence. People may need time to think about the question before formulating their answers.

11. Don't be content with just one answer. Ask, "What do the rest of you think?" or "Anything else?" until several people have given answers to the question.

12. Acknowledge all contributions. Try to be affirming whenever possible. Never reject an answer. If it is clearly off-base, ask, "Which verse led you to that conclusion?" or again, "What do the rest of you think?"

13. Don't expect every answer to be addressed to you, even though this will probably happen at first. As group members become more at ease, they will begin to truly interact with each other. This is one sign of healthy discussion.

14. Don't be afraid of controversy. It can be very stimulating. If you don't resolve an issue completely, don't be frustrated. Move on and keep it in mind for later. A subsequent study may solve the problem.

15. Periodically summarize what the group has said about the passage. This helps to draw together the various ideas mentioned and gives continuity to the study. But don't preach.

16. At the end of the Bible discussion you may want to allow group members a time of quiet to work on an idea under "Now or Later." Then discuss what you experienced. Or you may want to encourage group members to work on these ideas between meetings. Give an opportunity during the session for people to talk about what they are learning.

17. Conclude your time together with conversational prayer, adapting the prayer suggestion at the end of the study to your group. Ask for God's help in following through on the commitments you've made.

18. End on time.

Many more suggestions and helps are found in *How to Lead a LifeBuilder Study*.

Components of Small Groups

A healthy small group should do more than study the Bible. There are four components to consider as you structure your time together.

Nurture. Small groups help us to grow in our knowledge and love of God. Bible study is the key to making this happen and is the foundation of your small group.

Community. Small groups are a great place to develop deep friendships with other Christians. Allow time for informal interaction before and after each study. Plan activities and games that will help you get to know each other. Spend time having fun together—going on a picnic or cooking dinner together.

Worship and prayer. Your study will be enhanced by spending time praising God together in prayer or song. Pray for each other's needs— and keep track of how God is answering prayer in your group. Ask God to help you to apply what you are learning in your study.

Outreach. Reaching out to others can be a practical way of applying what you are learning, and it will keep your group from becoming self-focused. Host a series of evangelistic discussions for your friends or neighbors. Clean up the yard of an elderly friend. Serve at a soup kitchen together, or spend a day working in the community.

Many more suggestions and helps in each of these areas are found in the *Small Group Starter Kit.* You will also find information on building a small group. Reading through the starter kit will be worth your time.

Study 1. Hearing God's Call. Genesis 12.

Purpose: To learn to trust God when he asks us to leave what is familiar and to step out of our comfort zone.

Question 2. John Sailhamer writes, "Abraham, like Noah, marks a new beginning as well as a return to God's original plan of blessing 'all peoples on earth' (cf. 1:28). Notable is the frequent reiteration of God's 'blessing' throughout the narratives of Abraham and his descendants (12:1-3; 13:15-16; 15:5, 18; et al.). Abraham is here represented as a new Adam, the seed of Abraham as a second Adam, a new humanity. Those who 'bless' . . . him, God will bless; those who 'curse' . . . him, God will curse. The way of *life and blessing,* which was once marked by the 'tree of the knowledge of good and evil' (2:17) and then by the ark (7:23b), is now marked by identification with Abraham and his seed" (*The Zondervan NIV Bible Commentary,* vol. 1, *Old Testament,* ed. Kenneth L. Barker and John R. Kohlenberger III [Grand Rapids, Mich.: Zondervan, 1994], p. 21).

Question 4. The journey from Haran to Canaan is about five hundred miles and would take nearly a month. Yet the author of Genesis was far more interested in Abram's obedience than in the details of the journey. John Walton writes that Abraham "must decide whether to abandon his land in favor of the land Yahweh offers. He must decide whether to abandon what family he still has in favor of the family Yahweh promises (against all logic, given Sarai's infertility). He must decide whether to set aside his blessings, his inheritance, for the inheritance Yahweh describes. The initiative offers much but its cost is significant" (*Genesis*, NIV Application Commentary, ed. Terry Muck [Grand Rapids, Mich.: Zondervan, 2001], p. 392).

Questions 5-6. After traveling over five hundred miles to the Promised Land, Abram was told that it would be given to his offspring, even though it was now occupied by Canaanites. On a much smaller scale this would be like God taking you to a large mansion that is owned and lived in by another family and telling you, "This is the home I plan to give to your children." You would have to take this totally by faith, and what would you do in the meantime, especially since your previous home is now hundreds of miles away?

Question 8. Bruce Waltke writes, "Egypt would be appealing to Abraham, since he has no means for long-term food storage and Egypt has a dependable water supply in the Nile. . . . Since he receives no revelation to sojourn in Egypt (cf. 12:1; 26:2-6; 46:2-3), he is stepping out of the stones in God's will to find bread" (Bruce K. Waltke with Cathi J. Fredricks, *Genesis*, [Grand Rapids, Mich.: Zondervan, 2001], p. 213).

Question 9. Why did God punish Pharaoh, who acted in ignorance, instead of Abram, who acted in disobedience and unbelief? It seems clear that God was protecting not only Abram but also his promise to him of countless descendants. Later on in Genesis we discover that these descendants will come through both Abram and Sarai.

Study 2. Lift Up Your Eyes. Genesis 13.
Purpose: To help us follow Abram's example in trusting God to fulfill his promises.
Questions 3-4. It isn't clear from the narrative whether the land Lot chose was part of the Promised Land, on the edge of the Promised Land or just east of the Jordan River (see Waltke, *Genesis*, p. 221). Some commentators find fault with Abram for offering to Lot the land that God had promised Abram and his descendants. But the narrator of Genesis seems to approve of Abram's decision.

Question 6. *The NIV Study Bible* states that "the names of Sodom and Gomorrah became proverbial for vile wickedness and for divine judgment on sin. . . . Since the men of Sodom were known to be wicked (see v. 13), Lot was flirting with temptation by choosing to live near them. Contrast the actions of Abram (v. 18)" (*The NIV Study Bible*, ed. Kenneth Barker [Grand Rapids, Mich.: Zondervan, 1985], p. 26).

Question 9. In Galatians Paul made it clear that the promises of God are now given to the spiritual descendants of Abram—those who have faith—rather than to his physical descendants. Likewise, the blessings we receive are far greater than a physical land, physical descendants or material blessings. The ultimate blessing God gives is his Holy Spirit to live within us.

Study 3. Going to Battle. Genesis 14.

Purpose: To realize that God alone is our savior, provider and king.

Question 1. The word *king* appears twenty-eight times in this chapter. By naming the kings and their various countries, the author emphasizes Abram's greatness—and ultimately God's greatness over all earthly kings.

Question 4. After describing the power of the kings of the east and the weakness of the five Dead Sea kings, the author of Genesis emphasized that Abram was greater than all of them. Yet Abram himself later gave full credit to God.

Question 5. "Melchizedek is introduced as the king of Salem and is portrayed as the principle king of the region in that he receives a portion of the booty. Salem is generally considered to be Jerusalem, though early Christian evidence and the Madeba map associate it with Shechem" (John H. Walton and Victor H. Matthews, *The IVP Bible Background Commentary: Genesis—Deuteronomy* [Downers Grove, Ill.: InterVarsity Press, 1997], p. 40). Melchizedek's name means "king of righteousness."

Question 6. It is interesting to note that God is not mentioned throughout the first seventeen verses of this chapter—the time during which all of the battles take place. At first the author emphasized the power of the kings of the east and the weakness of the Dead Sea kings. Then he showed how Abram was more powerful than them all. But when Abram encountered Melchizedek, both of them acknowledged that "God Most

High . . . delivered your enemies into your hand" (Gen 14:18-20).

Question 8. "A contrast is established between Abraham's responses to the king of Salem and the king of Sodom. One is positive, the other negative. Lying behind Abraham's responses is the contrast between the offers of the two kings. The king of Salem brings 'bread and wine' as a priestly act and acknowledges that it was the 'God Most High, Creator of heaven and earth,' who delivered the adversaries into Abraham's hand. The king of Sodom offered Abraham the booty of the battle" (*Zondervan NIV Bible Commentary,* vol. 1, *Old Testament,* p. 23).

Study 4. The Covenant. Genesis 15.

Purpose: To increase our confidence in God's covenant faithfulness to us.

Question 1. In Genesis 13:16 the Lord had promised Abram, "I will make your offspring like the dust of the earth, so that if anyone could count the dust, then your offspring could be counted." And yet at this point in his life Abram had no children of his own, and evidently one of his servants, Eliezer of Damascus, would inherit Abram's estate. In Genesis 13:15 the Lord had also promised, "All the land that you see I will give to you and your offspring forever." So virtually all of the promises God had made about Abram's future were dependent on him having a son.

Questions 3-4. In Romans 4 the apostle Paul gives us very helpful insights into Abram's faith. Because Abram was so old, Paul says that "he faced the fact that his body was as good as dead—since he was about a hundred years old—and that Sarah's womb was also dead." Because Abram believed that God was able to bring life out of death, Paul encourages us to follow Abram's example: "The words, 'It was credited to him' were written not for him alone, but also for us, to whom God will credit righteousness—for us who believe in him who raised Jesus our Lord from the dead" (Rom 4:18-25).

Question 6. The Lord's actions of passing through the carcasses alone signifies that this promise was unconditional and dependent on God's faithfulness alone. "Second-millennium Hittite texts use a similar procedure for purification, while some first millennium Aramaic treatises use such a ritual for placing a curse on any violation of the treaty. Texts from Mari and Alalakh feature the killing of animals as part of the ceremony of making a treaty. Walking through this sacrificial pathway could be seen as a symbolic action enacting both the covenant's promises of land and a curse on the one who violates the promises, though interpreters have wondered what significance a self-curse could possibly have for God" (Walton and Matthews, *IVP Bible Background Commentary: Genensis—Deuteronomy*, pp. 41-42).

Question 7. Abram said to God in verse 8, "O Sovereign LORD, how can I know that I will gain possession of [the land]?" During Israel's enslavement in Egypt, they too would have wondered whether they would ever return to and possess the land God promised Abram. God assured Abram—and his descendants—that they would return to the land after their enslavement in Egypt. Also, after refusing to accept the spoils of war from the king of Sodom (14:22-24), Abram wondered whether God would, in fact, provide for him and his descendants. God assured him in 15:1 with the words "I am your shield and very great reward." To Abram's descendants he promised: "But I will punish the nation they serve as slaves, and afterward they will come out with great possessions" (v. 14).

Future generations of Israelites, including those who went through the seventy years of captivity in Babylon, would be encouraged by God's faithfulness to Abram and the fact that the Lord kept his promises and delivered Israel from Egypt. Readers would also see a deliberate link between the covenant God made with Abram and the covenant he would later make with Israel at Mount Sinai after delivering them from slavery in Egypt.

Study 5. Do-It-Yourself Religion. Genesis 16.
Purpose: To learn to wait on God when he doesn't answer our prayers or when his answer seems delayed.

Question 2. In Abram's day concubines did not have the full status of wives, and a wife could designate as her own the children borne by a concubine. Van der Torn comments, "The woman who remained childless not only ran the risk of being disdained, or worse, repudiated by her husband and in-laws, she also incurred the suspicion of indecent behavior. The gods surely had to have their reasons for withholding children. Consequently, we may safely assume that newly-wed who, as time elapsed perceived no signs pointing to pregnancy, was overcome by panic" (as quoted by Walton, *Genesis*, p. 447).

Question 3. In Genesis 15:4 the Lord had told Abram, "A son coming from your own body will be your heir." But it wasn't until Genesis 17:19 that the Lord explained, "Sarah will bear you a son, and you will call him Isaac. I will establish my covenant with him as an everlasting covenant for his descendants after him." The question remains, however, as to whether Abram followed Sarai's advice out of impatience and unbelief or whether he truly thought this was the way to fulfill God's promise. Waltke points out that the Hebrew for "agreed to what _____ said" occurs only in Genesis 3:17, where Adam agrees with Eve's suggestion to eat the forbidden fruit (Waltke, *Genesis*, p. 252). Encourage your group to wrestle with this question.

Question 6. Abram's actions may again reflect the customs of his day. According to the laws of Hammurabi, a wife could not sell her slave after her slave had borne a child for the wife's husband, but the wife could still treat her like a slave. Of course, this does not justify Sarai's mistreatment of Hagar, nor does it condone Abram's passive acceptance of this situation.

Questions 8-9. The narrator knew that Ishmael was also Abram's son and therefore would be blessed (see Gen 17:18, 20). But it is also clear in this passage that God both sees and hears those who are afflicted. In Hebrew the name "Ishmael" is a play on words with "has heard." Likewise, Hagar was amazed by the divine encounter and referred to the Lord as "the God who sees me" (16:13).

Study 6. Confirming the Covenant. Genesis 17.
Purpose: To discover how Abraham's obedience and trust can be models for us under the new covenant.

Question 1. These sections focus on the three divisions of covenant responsibility, beginning with God's (vv. 4-8), then Abraham's (vv. 9-14) and finally Sarah's (vv. 15-22).

Question 2. Twenty-four years had elapsed since God first promised Abram that he would have children. Compare 17:1 to 12:4. Thirteen years had passed since Ishmael's birth (16:16).

Question 3. "*God Almighty.* The Hebrew (*El-Shaddai*) perhaps means 'God, the Mountain One,' either highlighting the invincible power of God or referring to the mountains as God's symbolic home (see Ps 121:1). It was the special name by which God revealed himself to the patriarchs (see Ex 6:3). *Shaddai* occurs 31 times in the book of Job and 17 times in the rest of the Bible" (*The NIV Study Bible*, ed. Kenneth Barker [Grand Rapids, Mich.: Zondervan, 1985], p. 30).

Question 4. John Walton writes: "There are several statements made in the promises here that have not been previously revealed: He is to be the father of many nations, kings are to come from him, and the covenant is designated as an 'everlasting' covenant. In addition, there are name changes for Abram and Sarai, designation of circumcision as a sign, and reference to keeping the covenant. This is clearly an advancement of the covenant" (*Genesis*, p. 449).

Question 5. Wenham comments, "Whereas inaugurating the covenant was entirely the result of divine initiative, confirming it involves a human response, summed up in verse 1 by 'walk in my presence and be blameless' and spelled out in the demand to circumcise every male" (G. J. Wenham, *Genesis 16-50,* Word Biblical Commentary 2 [Dallas: Word, 1994], p. 20).

Question 6. This was one of the early indications that the Lord wanted to include in the covenant of blessing even those who are not physical descendants of Abram. In the New Testament Paul made it clear that the nations that come from Abram are not only his physical descendants but also—and ultimately—those who have his faith (Rom 4:16-17; Gal 3:15-19).

Question 7. Abraham was both astonished and amused at the idea that a husband who was one hundred years old would be able to have children with a wife who was ninety. Yet God promised that Sarah would not only have a son but also that "she [would] be the mother of nations; kings of peoples [would] come from her" (17:16). The names Sarai and Sarah both mean "princess."

Question 11. Abraham's obedience was both immediate ("that very day") and complete ("Every male in Abraham's household, including those born in his household or bought from a foreigner, was circumcised with him").

Study 7. Speaking Face to Face. Genesis 18.

Purpose: To discover that the transcendent God of the universe is also immanent and approachable.

Question 1. "The bowing, foot-washing, and offer of refreshment in the shade and a meal are all standard aspects of meticulous hospitality. Protocol required that the meal served to the guest exceed what was first offered. Thus, Abraham simply offers a meal, but what he orders prepared is freshly baked bread, a calf, and a mixture of milk and yogurt. . . . What is particularly generous here is the fresh meat, an item not normally found in their daily diet" (Walton, *Genesis*, p. 452).

Question 3. Ask your group how they would respond if they heard today that a ninety-year-old woman was planning to start a family with her one-hundred-year-old husband! As one person has said, Sarah would be the only mother who would be buying both Pampers and Depends at the same time.

Question 6. There is no record of schools in Israel until the late intertestamental period (Waltke, *Genesis*, p. 269), so the education of children took place through the home. Therefore, the Lord took this opportunity to model justice to Abraham so that he could "direct his children and his household after him to keep the way of the Lord by doing what is right and just" (Gen 18:19). This pattern of doing what is right and just could then be passed on from generation to generation as Abraham becomes "a great and powerful nation, and all nations on earth will be blessed through him" (v. 18).

Question 7. The way the Lord revealed himself to Abraham eventually reached its zenith in Jesus Christ, the God-man, who became incarnate not only during his time on earth but also for all eternity.

Question 8. Obviously, Abraham was not more righteous than the Lord. Instead, the Lord was using this situation to teach Abraham about compassion, justice and the need for intense prayer.

Study 8. Receiving the Promise. Genesis 21:1-21.

Purpose: To understand God's faithfulness, compassion and care.

Question 1. Surprisingly, after so many years of waiting for the birth of Isaac, after he is born the narrative focuses primarily on Hagar and Ishmael.

Question 2. Encourage your group to notice the words "as he had said," "what he had promised" and "at the very time God had promised him." The author of Genesis wants us to be clear that God was completely faithful in both his timing and his promises.

Question 4. Abraham's obedience is demonstrated by his giving his son the name "Isaac," which God had commanded in Genesis 17:19, and also by circumcising his son on the eighth day after his birth as God had commanded in Genesis 17:12. Sarah's delight is seen in her statement "God has brought me laughter, and everyone who hears about this will laugh with me," which is a play on words with the name Isaac, which means "laughter."

Question 7. Even though Ishmael had been sent away by Sarah because he mocked Abraham's heir, the narrative focuses on God's compassion toward Hagar and her son. The name Ishmael means "God hears," and this is seen throughout the story: "God heard the boy crying" (v. 17), and "Do not be afraid; God has heard the boy crying as he lies there" (v. 17). God also promised, "I will make him into a great nation" (v. 18), he provided Hagar and her son with water (v. 19), and the author of Genesis tells us that "God was with the boy as he grew up" (v. 20).

Question 8. When Abraham began to wonder why God had delayed so long in providing him with a son, he decided to take matters into his own hands rather than waiting for God's perfect timing. As a result, the son born to Hagar was merely the product of human effort. But Sarah's child required not only faith but also supernatural intervention by God. This story is meant to be an example to us today.

Study 9. The Ultimate Test. Genesis 22:1-19.

Purpose: To see how the most dramatic example of faith and obedience in the Old Testament can be a model for us today.

Question 1. In Hebrew the order of the words is slightly different, to heighten the drama: "Take your son": In a culture that valued a man by the number of his children, Abraham had to wait until he was one hundred years old to have Isaac—twenty-five years after the promise was originally given. After years of waiting and anguish, the son had finally come, and now God asked Abraham to sacrifice that son.

"Your only son": Technically speaking, this was not Abraham's only son. He also had Ishmael, the son of Hagar. But what God meant was that this was the son of promise—the one through whom all of God's promises to Abraham would be fulfilled: the promise of countless descendants. The promise that they would inherit the land of Canaan. The promise that all the nations of the earth would be blessed through Abraham's descendants. In other words, God was asking Abraham not only to sacrifice his son but also everything he ever hoped and dreamed of—his entire future.

"Whom you love—Isaac": I never knew how strong a parent's love could be until I had children. Abraham felt that strong, intense parental love for Isaac.

And "sacrifice him . . . as a burnt offering": The text spares us the details here, but in reality God is saying something shocking: "I want you to kill your son with a knife and burn his dead body."

Question 3. Abraham's obedience is incredible from the very beginning, when he got up early in the morning to carry out God's command, right up to the moment when he actually picked up the knife to slay his son. He never faltered. John Ortberg writes:

> This boy is his son, his only son, Isaac, whom he loves. And he ties up his legs, binds his arms, so there will be no struggle at the end. Then he picks up his son—bone of his bone and flesh of his flesh. He holds the same body that he held on the first day it came from Sarah's womb, the little body that he held to feed and bathe and rock and tell stories . . . the little body he would check on at night to make sure it was still breathing, and hold sometimes just to laugh at the sheer impossibility of it all. He holds that body one last time, then he places it on the altar, on the wood. Finally, he reaches toward heaven with the knife in his hand, to destroy with a single move the life he had created; and with it all his hope and joy and future. (John Ortberg, *The Life You've Always Wanted* [Grand Rapids, Mich.: Zondervan, 2002])

Abraham's obedience demonstrates that he cared more about God than anything—more than his son, more than his future and more than his own happiness. But Abraham's faith is even more remarkable. He could have said to God, "What kind of monster are you, asking me to kill my own son? That's what the pagan deities do! And why did you make all of those promises to me if you didn't intend to keep them? Now you're going to destroy both my son and my life." Yet he didn't respond that way. Notice verse 5: "He said to his servants, 'Stay here with the donkey while I and the boy go over there. We will worship and then we will come back to you.'" Look, too, at verses 7-8: "Isaac spoke up and said to his father Abraham, 'Father?' 'Yes, my son?' Abraham replied. 'The fire and wood are here,' Isaac said, 'but where is the lamb for the burnt offering?' Abraham answered, 'God himself will provide the lamb for the burnt offering, my son.'" Even at the last minute, when Abraham was picking up the knife to kill Isaac, he still had faith. The author of Hebrews writes, "Abraham reasoned that God could raise the dead, and figuratively speaking, he did receive Isaac back from death" (Heb 11:19).

Abraham never panicked. He never raised an angry fist at God. Why? Because he knew God. He knew the character of God. And so he knew he could entrust his life and the life of his son safely into God's care. That's faith!

Question 6. God, who knows all things, surely knew that Abraham feared him. But throughout Scripture the Lord emphasizes that true faith must manifest itself in actions in order to be complete.

Question 7. When we step out in obedience and faith, we experience God in a deeper way. Abraham had believed that God would spare Isaac, and he did. As a result, on that day Abraham had a deeper, richer experience of God's mercy and care. Abraham believed God would provide a lamb for the burnt offering. And he did! As a result, on that day Abraham had a deeper, richer experience of God's provision. Abraham also believed that God would be faithful to his incredible promises. And he was. As a result, on that day Abraham received a strong affirmation of God's blessing.

Question 8. When our faith is tested, we need to reflect on the great biblical examples of faith and how their lives were transformed: If Noah had not been willing to build the ark, he and his family never would have been delivered from the flood. If Joshua had not been willing to attack Jericho, he never would have seen the miracle of the walls collapsing outward. If Jesus had not been willing to be obedient to the point of death, he never would have experienced the resurrection we celebrate today. And if we are willing to step out of our comfort zones, to say "yes" to God when he tests our obedience and our faith—then we too will move to a higher, wider and deeper experience of God in our lives.

Jack Kuhatschek was formerly an executive vice president and publisher for Baker Publishing Group in Grand Rapids, Michigan. He is the author of many Bible study guides, including twelve in the LifeBuilder series, and the books Applying the Bible *and* The Superman Syndrome.